Just a Breath Away

KANIKA VERMA

Just a Breath Away by Kanika Verma

ISBN: 0692127763
ISBN-13: 978-0692127766

DEDICATION

To everyone who has touched my life,
directly or indirectly,
in good or bad ways,
and inspired me to express my emotions
and share those with the world.

"Give me thy hand, and hush awhile,
And turn those limpid eyes on mine,
And let me read there, love! thy inmost soul."

– Matthew Arnold

ACKNOWLEDGMENTS

This book is a work of fiction. Although any references to various events, people, and places are products of my imagination, I thank everyone who inspire me to write with passion and veracity. I am grateful to my parents, my family, my friends, and all the other people in my life who love me unconditionally and who believe in me and my capabilities.

……… but I also love

Yes, I am madly in love with you
But I also love
Butterflies in the garden
Raindrops on my hair
Petrichor
Smell of home-cooked food
The noise of the ocean waves
Budding flowers

Yes, I am madly in love with you
But I also love
Nurturing conversations with my mother
Communicating about life with my father
Hour long gossips with my high school bestie
Listening to my son's stories
Discussing research with my colleagues

Yes, I am madly in love with you
But I also love
Creating art
Composing poetry
Writing research papers
Scribbling my thoughts
Reading about life
Cooking with my partner
Dancing with strangers
Eating with friends
Watching films
Travelling to different places
Preparing class lectures
Learning with my students
Doing this today and that tomorrow
Pampering myself
And appreciating others

Yes, I am madly in love with you
But I also love
Crazy conversations with the roadside guy
Flirting with the handsome dude I met at the club
Getting attracted to the boy I saw at the beach
Falling for the rock star I got a selfie with

Yes, I am madly in love with you
But I also love

Questioning life
Seeking answers
Losing sight
And finding my way back home

What went wrong?

After months of
amorous attractions,
cupid flirting
and passionate conversations
Frequent exchanges of verbal and
textual sensory sweet-nothings
Moments when he said,
"Get your chap stick ready,
I will run your lips dry"
Times when I blushed reading his texts
on my bright phone screen
"I can't wait to love you my love"
After days of gracious flattering
and romantic appreciation of
my beauty and intellect
Points when he emphasized
using the adjective
"dammmnnnnnn"
before any word to compliment
my charm was necessary

The night before our meeting
he strategically warned me
"Beware girl, get your pen
and paper ready.
You are going to create
a beautiful poem tomorrow
from our lovemaking"
And I spent the night thinking about
our rendezvous tomorrow night
When every fraction of his
skin will caress mine
and every inch of his
body will fondle mine
and every breath of his
soul will rhythm with mine
and every beat of his
heart will skip with mine
and every glance of his
eyes will intoxicate with mine

On that chilly December night
we deliberately cancelled
all our outdoor plans

of watching a movie
and eating dinner at a fancy restaurant
To spend intimate time with each other
in the coziness of his bedroom
in the warmth of each other's arms.

After hours of intense kissing
blissful moments of fondling
ardent flashes of glaring
He went down on me
and I was ignited by orgasmic glimmers
Then I took my turn to
provide sensual frenzy
to this charismatic man
Minutes of rubbing
more minutes of stroking
more and more minutes of fellatio
But his phallus didn't even reach a point
to claim the lowest place
on the scale of hardness

"What is it you feel?"
I asked him
"What turns you on?"

And he said
"You turn me on"

Lovemaking

It happened when the
night was pleasant,
It happened when
no one was present.

It happened when
everything was bright,
And I caught
his pleasing sight.

He was in a merry mood,
And talked and talked for good.

I saw him coming
towards me,
To lessen my curiosity,
I tightly held my knee.

He was beside me the next moment,
His words strengthened the romaunt.

Together we were
on the bed,
I blushed and my
cheeks turned red.

He asked me to
come closer,
Every second, the distance
between us grew lesser.

With me was
my cutie-pie,
Who fondled me
under the endless sky.

My heart gave a sigh,
while I was feeling shy.

I hid my face
with a pillow,
With the beauty
of a silent willow.

My countenance was covered
with the falling hair,
He removed them to put
a glance on the blushing fair.

I found he was
growing naughty,
When his fingers began
to dance on my body.

His one touch on my bosom
had a tickling effect,
I felt uneasy in the beginning,
but I enjoyed the rest.

When his lips were
playing on my neck,
His hands began to
stroll on my back.

The movement of my
body was serpentine,
The drink of his eyes
was nectar divine.

His eyes began to scintillate,
I cuddled him before it was too late.

One truth beyond all lies,
I loved his infinite eyes.

His aphrodisiac game was a clue,
Was it a dream come true?

Slowly and softly
I slithered under him
For the next few seconds
my imagination became dim.

My nails dug
into his skin,
This time, his lips
struggled with my chin.

In his arms, I hid,
When I was unable

to get myself rid.

I realized, I chose
the wrong place,
When his lips were
again on my face.

His one kiss gave the
wonders of a thousand bliss.

I tried to stop him,
but it was all in vain,
One more smack
increased my pain.

My lips grew rosy,
His hug made me cozy.

Soul meets soul
on lovers' lips,
Was it a dream of those
long never-ending kips?

During those animate moments,
he captured my spell,
Since then, my every
breath is exuding his smell.

In the game of love,
he is intrepid,
Like the true
epitome of Cupid.

He is my angel, my darling,
Without him, my existence
has no meaning,
The process of love making,
I am learning,
I am his angel, his darling.
With his love,
in his shade,
I would never let these
lovely moments fade.

Dr. Love

People call him Dr. Love
He deals with hearts
and works with momentary emotions
He sweats feelings
and labors fondness
He attracts souls
and draws bodies
with cupid ease

People call him Dr. Love
He chased me
with fine words
and amorous eyes
He captivated me
with boundless affection
and the unfair mention of devotion
He drank nectars
of my physical pleasures
and flowing waterfalls
of my coveted pristine beauty
He devoured my succulent bosom
and blushing curvy flesh

People call him Dr. Love
He underuses love to heal me
He asked me to build bridges
between us
but erected water walls
He forgets to add emotions
in the envelope to
my heart's address
He devotes no time
in comprehending
my flowing feelings

People call him Dr. Love
Not just in vain
he heals tired souls
and nurtures longing spirits
I want to explore
more and more,
how he mends wounded hearts
and not just adores decorated bodies
How he unlocks emotional depths

and not only unbutton laced blouses

People call him Dr. Love
Is he masking
fears of attachment
Are the pains of longing
clouding his inner desires
Are the hollow confusions
of social rights and wrongs
limiting his moves
For it is hard not to love me,
and he will regret
not letting me love him enough
I am stubborn to believe
that when in doubt
love is always the right answer

People call him Dr. Love
I know he loves loving freely
For his coldness
never bothers me
His innocent ignorance
hardly angers me
His innocuous carelessness
seldom perplexes me
If he is Dr. Love,
I am his patient

People call him Dr. Love
I always doubted
that he is a merchant like me,
I am now convinced
That he deals in hearts
and I deal in words

Empathy for my husband

After hours of carefree
dancing at a party
The first thing
that charming stranger
asked me was
if I was single.
I firmly said *"No"*
"It never hurts to ask"
He candidly replied.

He began a series of
amorous messages
and playful chats,
gracious flattery
mixed with harmless flirting.

To curb my persistent hesitation
He would say,
"All it takes is one moment
to fall for someone"
To my *"I am married"* rants
He would confidently express
his self-created and
self-accepted challenge,
"It is no fun to park in
an open parking spot"

Was I enjoying giving in
to the pleasures of life
and respectful attention?
to the blissful moments
and joyous compliments?
to the sensual appealing
that were feeding my
unquenchable curiosity
of my lifelong quest
to uncover the mystery of love,
that no psychological outline
or philosophical framework
or mathematical formula
or scientific experiment
has yet sufficiently explained

Months passed by
and he suddenly
becomes uninterested
and feels lack of intimacy
He does not get excited
any more
With my touch or words
Not because
something went wrong
between us

He now feels
sudden bursts of empathy
and compassion
for my husband
whom he never met.
He now becomes a self-assigned
judge of my morality,
of which he previously
enjoyed every second.

Love Marks

When we met, I felt that
my heart has known your soul
before your lips tasted my skin
my eyes have fathomed your depths
before your hands grasped my body

You left the marks
of love on my body
My lips' cracks needed
no warmth on the night it snowed
My erected nipples peeked
through my winter jacket
My bruised body resembled
an active battlefield
People read eyes and forms
And I can't hide your love marks

I am trying to find
the marks deeper than the skin
Leave your imprints on my soul
Make your footprints on my heart
Make my smile the haven that
you would want to visit again
Let my eyes solve your life's mysteries
My body is not the only place
you want to enter
I present my body to you and
honor your's as a privilege

You traced the outline of my lips with yours
You measured the size of my breasts with your palms
You drew grids on my torso with your fingertips
Your hands made thousand promises to my flesh

Body is the least naked part of me
Make your way through my soul to see me nude
Untangle the nerves in my brain to see me bare
Rip the layers on my heart to see me unclothed

Lying with words

I am a geographer
I study maps
and play with atlases
I love Earth's layouts
Lines drawn in different fashions
Strokes depicting physical
and human features
Grids showing streets
Arcs depicting rivers

Scale defines perspective
A dot in a travel book
shows a pub in Oxford's enclave
The same circle in an encyclopedia
wraps up entire London
with a black spot

Borders depict political motives
Boundaries show territorial hegemony
Kashmir is burning on the ground
Burdened lines on the paper
bring tears in the paradise
color the valley red
paint souls in Pakistan blue
set hearts in India ablaze

I learned in academia
that you can lie with maps
Little did I know
that you can also lie with words
until I started writing poetry

You are always with me

You are always with me
I feel you in my first morning breath
I see you in my late night's dream
You tease me in the lazy siesta
You sweat me in the day's labor

You are always with me
I taste you in my luscious breakfast
I savor you in my warm lunch
You give me warmth with my cup of tea
You satiate me in the minimal supper

You are always with me
I house you in my bright eyes
I tangle you tight in my shiny locks
You turn my cheeks rosy on cold winter mornings
You curve my lips in myriad arcs

You are always with me
I inhale you in the gentle breeze
I drink you in the sweet rain drops
You shine in me when the sun rays kiss my body
You comfort me when the moonlight caresses me to sleep

You are always with me
I sing you in maudlin songs
I dance you in utopian moves
You become colors on my white canvas
You become words on my bare paper

Company of men

I am independent and strong
needing regular doses of romance
Those currents of intimacy and flattery
may not surge from the same man

Love is passionately beautiful
it should happen every second
not just everyday
I may not rise in love with the same man

I have a talent for happiness
the art of making something out of nothing
Those joy flowers of sunshine smiles
may not blossom in the soil of the same man

I seek utopian pleasure
in small moments of life
Those strands of orgasmic magic
may not culminate in the arms of the same man

I enjoy conversations of depth and intellect
planting seeds of fascinating ideas
Those exchange of thoughtful words
may not transpire in the company of the same man

Incomplete poem

You are the poem
always present in my heart
I never found
the words to create you in my life
I never detected
the lines to manifest you in my world

Phrases lingered in my mind
and teased my psyche
I could never connect the dots
to trace the circle and trap you in

Blank paper of my solitary life
colorless and quiet
Words hidden behind the social veils of shame
never touched my open paper

Some traitor passions
changing perspectives
to fit cultural norms
never decorated my failing paper

Some aged desires
lost in memory
washed away with tears
without impregnating my barren paper

Some cacophonic sounds
disturbed the silence
disrupted the melody
of my quiet paper

Experiences

I made a choice
In the moment
That was my present
That was happening now
That moment became mine

The moment it passed
It became an experience
And then I wondered
This experience was good?
Not so good?

This is life
Nothing less
Nothing more

Expiry Date

Memories do not have an expiry date,
Feelings do.

Love does not have an expiry date,
Relationships do.

Imagination does not have an expiry date,
Ideas do.

Gestures do not have an expiry date,
Promises do.

Choices do not have an expiry date,
Rules do.

Life does not have an expiry date,
We do.

Fire and Water

I hold huge fire inside me
Do not come near me
For you will get burned

But when you come near me
The same fire
Turns into
Waters full of love

Still do not come near me
For you will
Keep floating
In those waters
And never reach
Where you should be

Home

Rummaging through the pages of my atlas
My mental maps collected over the years
I wondered where is home

I felt home is where
I breathed life for the first time
hopping and growing
in the comfort of my parents' arms

I thought I found home in his heart
Cuddling in his amorous touch
I gave new definitions to love
And boundaries to my body

I realized I kissed home
when I gave birth to another life
and held my reflection in my arms
and wandered afar in his innocent smiles

There were times when I mistook
money and work to be my home
and liberty and party to unhome me
when I burn out of my desire to find abode

Home is also where
I spent twenty-five years of my life
Home is also where
twenty-five minutes gave me the real taste of life

Home is also where
he said "*Feel like home*"
Home is also in my thoughts
that give me wings to fly

I also found home in your eyes
And in his heart
I also found home in your words
And in his touch

Sitting in the comforts of my home
When I felt homelessness
I wondered where is home
Trotting from one home to another
I am still searching home

I am…..

I am strong like mountains
I am fragile like winds

I am quiet like deserts
I am chirpy like birds

I am deep like soil
I am open like flowers

I am dense like forests
I am sparse like rainbows

I am loose like rivers
I am restricted like trees

I sparkle in the sunshine
I blush in the shade

I am smooth like marble
I am rough like storm

I am dark like coal
I am clear like diamonds

I am busy like cities
I am idle like oceans

I am permanent like energy
I am temporary like everything else

If you were a flower

If you were a flower
You'd be a dandelion
Your hair swift in beautiful arcs
and drift in gentle waves
Your beauty oh so pure and gentle
A touch would disarray your petals

I would sit for hours and watch
as you abandon your roots
and cross the fields
jump over bushes
and float in streams
soar high and settle down

You play and laugh
with the blissful innocence
and yet your naughty gestures
make me blush
and turn my cheeks wintery red

I watch fondly
as you fly and float
and rest and roar
I wait patiently
for you to land in my lap
and let me fondle you

I will drive you
into the countryside
Where your haunting beauty
will fade the lunar charm on a full moon night
We will sit next to a bubbling spring
and stare at the stars
I will admire as you
do your dance
And then set you free
so you flutter
to the open blue skies
and the lush green fields
where you belong

It takes time

It is not about my dreams
I want to be a traveler
It takes time to go back home

It is not about possession
I want to nurture love
It takes time for a flower to bloom

It is not about her body
I want to reach her soul
It takes time to travel long distances

It is not about the moon's power
I want to witness nature
It takes time for a tide to rise

It is not about the questions
I want to live the uncertainties
It takes time to find answers

It is not about fame
I want to give expression
It takes time to write a poem

Liberty

He picked up
his packed bags
and stood at the doorstep

He hugged her
Waved goodbye and said,
"*Now you'll be free*"
She said, "*I am always free*
Those who are independent
in the mind are always free,
Those who only believe in physical freedom
have not known what liberty is"

My home America

Do not alienate me
from my home
because my homeland
is not same as yours
I long for the relations
my sweat nurtured for years
in the land that I call
home now, my America

Fleeing the terror
in my homeland,
I cried, "*Take me, I am tired*
Take me, I am exhausted
Take me, I am yearning to breathe."
Your statue of liberty
aired my choked breaths
Your land of the free
welcomed my fears
Your water of the sovereign
embraced my tears

Your horizons yearned
for my approaching shadow
Do not let your broken borders
dread the nearing steps of my kin
Your soil absorbed
my labor and love
Do not allow your fixed frontiers
fear the faith that my clan brings in

I call the God by a different name
But I fed the homeless in your church
My ethnic color doesn't match your hue
But I respect your red, white, and blue
I speak a different language
But I learned English to understand you
Do not keep my people
far from this cordial crowd

There are millions of sons
of my faith born in your soil
of the sailors and
slaves who landed
of the refugees and

romeos who romanced
of the farmers and
fryers who fed
of the soldiers and
veterans who protected
These sons built America

There are millions of daughters
of my color raised in your dust
by the scientists and
singers who created
by the inventors and
investors who developed
by the educators and
entrepreneurs who inspired
by the poets and
painters who dreamed
These daughters evolved America

America

I embrace this land of immigration
Does America love my integration?

I embody this land of diversity
Does America love my ethnicity?

I respect this land of liberty
Does America love my creativity?

I adopt this land of justice
Does America love my substance?

I understand this land of history
Does America love my story?

I accept this land of opportunity
Does America love my community?

I espouse this land of dollar
Does America love my labor?

I integrate this land of red, white, and blue
Does America love my hue?

I absorb this land of hurry
Does America love my curry?

I love this land as a melting pot
Does America love my thought?

All who came

All who came
talked with me
in different tones

All who came
touched me
with different forces

All who came
entered me
in different dimensions

All who came
stroked my heart
with different emotions

All who came
embraced my soul
with different meanings

All who came
spent on me
in different magnitudes

All who came
taught me
with different perspectives

Earthed

The water calls me to wash my sins,
and to nourish my roots

The air calls me to dust my guilt,
and to sail my desires

The fire calls me to burn my evils,
and to fuel my passions

The earth calls me to bury my offenses,
and to nurture my ambitions

The space calls me to free me of my burdens,
and to energize my soul

Night

I want someone to hug me tight
When I am going to embrace the night

I want someone to put me to sleep
When I am going to forget the world deep

I want someone to hold my body
When I am going to get my dreams ready

I want someone to kiss me long
When I am going to sing the slumber song

Need

Give me your sorrows
I need that glow
for your absence
removes the sun shine on my body

In the vacuum of your words,
the words stop coming to me

The universe tells me
that you are thinking about me
but life's callings keep you from me

and then I wonder
am I one of your life's callings?

For you told me
that you need me

and I am there when you do
when you come to me to find physical pleasure
when you come to me to seek emotional dependency
when you come to me to nurture spiritual pursuit
when you come to me to attain social celebration
when you come to me to unburden
when you come to me to desire
when you come to me to let loose
when you come to me to escape
when you come to me to let go
when you come to me to share the overflowing
when you come to me to unwind
when you come to me to feel the difference
when you come to me to discover a new emotion
over and over again

And then I pause and think
I, too, need you
to come to you to find physical pleasure
to seek emotional dependency
to nurture spiritual pursuit
to attain social celebration
to unburden
to desire
to let loose
to escape

to let go
to share the overflowing
to unwind
to feel the difference
to discover a new emotion
over and over again

and to channelize my energies
towards love

Love with the eyes

I hate your eyes
because no matter
how deep I dive
I see nothing
I love your eyes
because no matter
how deep I dive
I feel everything

I want to enter your eyes
let me see the hidden treasures
let me feel the gaps that deceive
I do not want to enter your eyes
for I do not wish to disturb the tranquility
for I want to be enchanted forever

I hate the distance between us
for it keeps me away from you
I love the distance between us
for it gives me chances to come closer to you

Let me dive into your eyes
and connect to your soul

Promises in Solitude

We began with promises where
no part of my body will be
untouched by your caress
no part of my heart
unloved by your warmth
no part of my soul
unaddressed by your words
no part of my life
unlived with your presence

Parts of me will touch
parts of you
You only show me
what I can absorb
I only give you
what you can contain
And yet we deliver each other
Promises of a lifetime
That may not even see
four seasons of a year

When you swim in my shallow waters
and forget the deep oceans that i harbor
When you cannot fathom the throbs that you hear
are beats from your heart or mine

You are only listening to words
that trigger sexual bells in your vitals
and arouse orgasmic beats in your senses

I am not who I look on the surface
My flesh has sparkles
and my body oozes seduction
But I nurture miracles in my laughter
I hide surprises in my smiles
I carry wonders in my words

My hungry heart
craves for the unknown
Your eager soul
desires for the inaccessible
Our voracious bodies
search for the solitude
Do not come to meet me when I die

Befriend the indomitable me when I am alive
Body is not that medium
through which you reach me
Read what I write to know me

Wanderer

It's hard to settle with one notion
It's fun to be in motion

It's hard to be in one place for a long time
It's fun to try new things in line

It's hard to attach to an idea or soul
It's fun to see things and people roll

It's hard to see people get attached to things
It's fun to fly with open wings

It's hard to be happy here
It's fun to visualize how joy would look like there

It's hard to be in captivity
It's fun to engage in creativity

We are energy

I do not believe in religion
I am not a Hindu
You are not a Muslim
We are humans

I do not believe in caste
I am not a Kshatriya
You are not a Sudra
We are culture

I do not believe in color
I am not brown
You are not white
We are melanin

I do not believe in borders
I am not an Indian
You are not an American
We are universal

I do not believe in politics
I am not a democrat
You are not a republican
We are perspectives

I do not believe in language
I do not speak Hindi
You do not speak English
We are understanding

I do not believe in age
I am not young
You are not old
We are life

I do not believe in appearance
I am not sexy
You are not ugly
We are beautiful

I do not believe in economy
I am not poor
You are not rich
We are abundance

I do not believe in relationships
I am not straight
You are not gay
We are love

I do not believe in marriage
I am not wife
You are not husband
We are companions

I do not believe in hierarchy
I am not a leader
You are not a disciple
We are work

I do not believe in competition
I am not a winner
You are not a loser
We are symbiosis

I do not believe in education
I am not an artist
You are not a scientist
We are creativity

I do not believe in war
I am not civilized
You are not barbaric
We are progress

I do not believe in sex
I am not female
You are not male
We are bodies

I do not believe in time
I am not future
You are not past
We are now

I do not believe in inertia
I am not origin
You are not destination
We are journey

I do not believe in magnitude
I am not small
You are not big
We are dimensions

I do not believe in dichotomy
I am not right
You are not wrong
We are experiences

Your eyes

Your eyes tell me
how beautiful I am

Your eyes speak untold tales
of inaccessible lands

Your eyes captivate me
and guide me to your soul

Your eyes signal me
what to say and what to behold

Your eyes hint me
about mysteries to be solved

Your eyes reveal myriads
yet hide infinites

Let me dive deep into your eyes
dig deep into your soul

Let me search deep into your thoughts
and let me love you through your eyes

Time and Magnitude

Do not disgrace my relationships.

How do you have more reliance
in your temporary relation of twenty-five years
than in my temporary relation of twenty-five months?

How do you have more life
in your temporary relation of twenty-five months
than in my temporary relation of twenty-five weeks?

How are your experiences
from your temporary relation of twenty-five weeks
more profound than from my temporary relation of twenty-five days?

How do you have more love
in your temporary relation of twenty-five days
than in my temporary relation of twenty-five hours?

How is your conversation more meaningful
in your temporary relation of twenty-five hours
than in my temporary relation of twenty-five minutes?

How is your connection deeper
in your temporary relation of twenty-five minutes
than in my temporary relation of twenty-five seconds?

Unfinished conversations

Some unfinished conversations
say a lot

Some unfinished conversations
show great depths

Some unfinished conversations
are completed with mere glances

Some unfinished conversations
finish relationships
Some too soon, some too late

Some unfinished conversations
prolong relationships
indefinitely

Some unfinished conversations
transcend you to another dimensions

Some unfinished conversations
bring complete bliss

Some unfinished conversations
are never finished

You or I?

I kept asking
"Do I belong to you?"

Then the realization came in my being
I belong to none but myself

My feelings are for none but to nurture my own soul
My love is for none but to quench my own longings
My care is for none but to fulfill my own demands
My attention is for none but to satiate my own desires

then why am I looking for answers in you?

A touch of belongingness

My hands
caress my bosom
when I sleep

It gives me personal touch
It gives me security
It fulfills my isolation
It gives me company

My touch on my bosom
reassures my being
That I am there for myself

Attraction

I am attracted to you for the way you touch me
And you for the way you talk to me
And you for the way you tease me
And you for the way you kiss me
And you for the way you give me pleasure
And you for the way you take care of me
And you for the way you never get tired of me
And you for the way you understand me
And you for the way you provide for me
And you for the way you choose me to pour love

I am attracted to you for the way you share your body with me
And you for the way you share your time with me
And you for the way you share your emotions with me
And you for the way you share your resources with me

This attraction is not about you
It is about how you treat me
to explore the different ways
love touches me

Rendezvous

We will meet in the forest
Where the tree canopy will provide shade and cool
And all the wild will shy away from the lioness in you

We will meet at the ocean
Where the noisy waves will caress our warm bodies
And the scattered sand will sparkle on your locks

We will meet in the mountains
Where the cold pristine snow will get spotted by our aimless stride
And the serene valleys will echo our amorous songs

We will meet in a city
Where no one knows us
And the lazy strangers will strengthen our passion with their innocent smiles

We will meet in a library
Where the silence of the deserted aisles will be disturbed by our exchanges
And the abandoned books will crave for our touch

Resilience

I kept saying
this is not my fault

I kept reassuring
I won't feel like this forever

I kept comforting
this does not affect every area of my life

Uninvited

All the glances
in the party
made me feel
that I was uninvited

The only look
the look of your eyes
was the familiar look
the warm welcoming look

We exchanged words
without talking
We planned
without arranging

We hugged
without touching
We kissed
without tasting

Your warm gestures
gave me pride and confidence
Your caring remarks
told everyone that I was not uninvited

Survival

The entire room
felt empty
The doors, walls
and the windows
started shouting
"*You do not belong here*"

I went out
to escape the confinement
to embrace the nature
for nature never discriminates
The powerful nature tried
to overpower the fragile me

The clouds were crushing me
The winds were blowing me away
The oceans were engulfing me
The rivers were drowning me
The mountains were scorning me
The forests were puzzling me

The light in me refused to be extinguished
by the fierce raindrops of misery
The hope in me declined to get burnt
by the blazing lava of obstacles
The strength in me denied to be drowned
in the inimical streams of anguish

Senses

Your eyes orgasmed
with my pleasant sight
Your ears thrilled
with my utopian words
Then your skin, tongue, and nose
wanted to dive into my euphoria

You welcomed me into your life
with unlimited access
though there were social barriers
and emotional obstacles
You were in a hurry
to consume me

You were impatient
to dive in me
Yet you were afraid of opening up
You were scared of sharing
You were apprehensive of getting attached
You were afraid of getting hurt

You reassured me of your love....
we will sail the ocean of emotions
we will surrender to the desires of our bodies
we will talk the notions of life
we will scale the mountains of social restrictions
we will dance to the songs of joy

After you have had me
you have slowed down
The fire of impatience has extinguished
The burning of haste is stagnant
You said I was irresistible
What are you suspicious of now?

You have satiated yourself with the physical me
There are galaxies of the unknown in the emotional me
There are diamonds in my inaccessible spiritual mines
There is the lucrative oil if you dig deep in the social me
There is the romantic oasis in my passionate deserts
There is the confluence of rivers in my infinite oceans

Do not stop my love
Do not restrict my honey

Do not only cater to your skin
Keep satiating your sense of hearing
Keep nurturing what you see and smell
Do not only let your tongue and lips savor me

The physical me is succulent….
indulge in the words that I speak
dream in the thoughts that I create
dance in the rhythms that I sing
float on the clouds that I aim
drench in the rains that I covet

I keep the flame of desire in me ablaze
You are drifting towards me each moment
And each moment will pass
either with you or in waiting for you
In this moment, you are somewhere else
spreading love with your senses

Unconventional

What am I to do
with so much love
that bleeds from my skin
that pours from my heart
that evaporates from my soul

There are many takers…..
some till my last breath
some till theirs
some come and go
some only want what bleeds
some want what evaporates or pours
some all of it
some want this but get that
some receive it from a distance
some come too close

I will journey on….

not to seek the takers
but to fill the empty vessels
not to pour in the flooded terrains
but to rain in the droughts
not to plant in the forests
but to grow in the deserts
not to confine the oceans
but to liberate the lakes
not to scale the mountains
but to uplift the valleys

To love someone is easy
To fulfill that love takes real courage

my love knows no barriers
seeks you who fulfill promised love
my love knows no boundaries
seeks you who seek unconventional ways

Silent Words

I am unable to finish
the epistle to my sweetheart
Words, wet with tears, fall too short
to express my wounded heart

when my heavy tears recede
the feelings might turn into words
my silence turns the paper into a grave
the words die with pain while landing

My alien eyes try to say it all
why are feelings dependent on mere words
He comprehended each signal from my deep eyes
Now he listens only to hollow words

I am waiting to write
But each moment is slipping away
like melting ice in warm hands
my words are not faithful anymore

I am waiting for my tears to dry
But my stubborn eyes don't tire
like a snow-fed perennial river
my eyes are not faithful anymore

My voice faints before reaching him
The lamp of my love never extinguishes
He will keep looking for words
I will keep expressing through silence

Sin

We all have sinned
My sins are different than yours
You found pleasure in the high reaches of the mountains
I gained liberty in the depths of the ocean

Sin is an illusion
And so is virtue
Social mores are deceptive
And normal is a delusion

Who could define the range of sin
Or set the bounds of sacred
I saw beauty in loving unconventionally
You found joy in pristine kisses

Synonym of Love

I have been in situations
where jealousy equaled love
I have been stuck in relations
where possession measured love
I have glimpsed incidents
where physical presence expressed love

I have witnessed moments
where approval qualified love
I have observed scenes
where acceptance signaled love
I have viewed settings
where appreciation indicates love

It is hard to narrow down
any human feeling
that parallels love
The most incomprehensible thing
about love is that
it is comprehensible

Gratitude

Thank you for seeing the light in me
when there is darkness around

Thank you for finding love in me
when there is hatred around

Thank you for accepting me
when there is rejection around

Thank you for having faith in me
when there is despair around

Thank you for holding onto me
when people are moving on around

Questions

The winds that are touching your cheeks
have caressed my body
and transported my fragrance to you

The flowers that you picked
for your beloved
were nurtured with my sweat

The waters from the stream
that quench your thirst
have washed my sins

The damsels that you flirt with
have played with me
in the idle streets of this busy city

The people you encounter
will pose questions……
busy and idle spirits

happy and sad humans
contended and hungry souls
beautiful and unattractive bodies

queries that come straight from my heart
doubts that weaken my trust in our bond
uncertainties that cloud my vision of our tomorrow

The people I meet and
how I reciprocate their feelings
will answer the questions I have for you

Where are you?

Where are those eyes that were constantly looking for me?
Where are those hands that were holding me tight?

Where are those smiles that would make me feel naughty?
Where are those laughs that would kindle the love in me?

Where is the soul that wanted to be with me every second?
Where is the touch that fires the passion in me?

Where are those arms that would comfort me?
Where are those hugs that warmed my soul?

Where are those roads that witnessed our animate drives?
Where is the waterfall that witnessed our first kiss?

Where is the ocean that gave us comfort in the stormy night?
Where are those stars that blanketed us in the seductive dark?

Where are those words that would extoll me day and night?
Where are those glances that didn't need words to express?

Why I write

I write for the girls
who are confused between
flirting and flattery
love and lust
dreams and desires
bodies and boundaries

I write for the mothers
who sacrifice their passions
to nurture their kids

I write for the achievers
who are proud to work hard
and earn a coveted life

I write for the dreamers
who carry a vision in their souls
to give meaning to existence

I write for the lovers
whose hearts burn and sing
for their unfulfilled desires

I write to express
what hurts our souls,
what brings tears to our eyes,
what stirs our happiness,
what fuels our passions,
what drives us wild

I write to cry
I write to dance
I write to sing
I write to shout
I write to question
I write to love

"You can never know anyone as completely as you want.
But that's okay, love is better."

– Caroline Paul

ABOUT THE AUTHOR

With more than 8 years of experience in education, Dr. Kanika Verma has received 12 awards and several other recognitions for her research, teaching, and service. She teaches geography and statistics to undergraduate students, and has taught at Texas State University and Texas Christian University. Her research is focused on geospatial thinking and academic learning of students. She has completed research projects on classroom pedagogy and active learning. She has presented her award-winning research studies at more than 40 professional conferences. She has mentored several students and positively impacted their academic achievements. She regularly organizes art of writing programs for school and college students and professional writing workshops for adults.

Kanika has authored five peer-reviewed journal articles, two peer-reviewed book chapters, and one peer-reviewed e-book. She also serves on review and judging panels of such organizations as Geography Education Specialty Group and Ethnic Geography Specialty Group of the American Association of Geographers (AAG), National Council for Geographic Education (NCGE), Society for the Study of Social Problems (SSSP), Race, Ethnicity, and Place (REP), and Inspiration Masters. She holds various officer positions in the International Women's Club (IWC), All India Foundation for Peace and Disaster Management (AIFPDM), and India International Intellectual Society (IIIS). Kanika is the area representative for the Dallas-Fort Worth metropolitan region (North Prairie and Pines) for *Youth For Understanding* (YFU), an international educational exchange organization, where she mentors exchange students coming to the U.S. from all over the world by leading training sessions.

Apart from academic and professional writing, Kanika writes poetry in English and Hindi. Her Hindi poems have been published in several literary magazines. Few of her Hindi poems are in the process of being composed into songs. Kanika's other interests include reading, traveling, and dancing.